T0159091

Rainy Day Haikus

with a

Sprinkling of Scripture

Rainy Day Haikus
with a
Sprinkling of Scripture

Written and Illustrated by
Susan Steele

authorHOUSE®

AuthorHouse™
1663 Liberty Drive
Bloomington, IN 47403
www.authorhouse.com
Phone: 1-800-839-8640

I See You . . . Writing, a division of:
I See You . . . Ministry (recognizing the faithful)
Inspired of the Holy Spirit, created by Susan Steele

Published by AuthorHouse   09/26/2012

ISBN: 978-1-4772-6501-7 (sc)
ISBN: 978-1-4772-6500-0 (e)

Library of Congress Control Number: 2012916039

My beloved spoke, and

said to me:

"Rise up, my love, my fair one,

And come away.

For lo, the winter is past,

The rain is over and gone.

The flowers appear on the earth;

The time of singing has come.

Song of Solomon 2:10-12a

This book is dedicated to the
Lord Jesus Christ

. . . who gives us rainy days . . .

To my daughter Emily Sue

. . . who loves a rainy day . . .

And to my son Jered

. . . who has experienced rainy days in a
myriad of countries . . .

Acknowledgments:

To Jesus—My Lord and Savior. Thank You for loving me, inspiring me, and molding me into the person I am today. All glory, praise, and honor for this project belongs to You. Be magnified in my life!

To my Mom—Thank you for proofreading almost every paper I've ever written, including this book. You have always been my greatest (earthly) cheerleader. I love you.

To my Daughter—Thank you for critiquing the artwork. Your comments and insight are invaluable to me. You are a precious Gift from God!

To my David—God knows who you are. You are the stuff of which dreams are made.

Preface

Initially, I had asked a couple of very artistic people if they would be willing to do the art work for this book. Much to my consternation, each of them politely declined. So, I then decided to try my own hand at being creative. With colored pencils in hand, I made an attempt to create what I thought would be the final artwork for *Rainy Day Haikus with a Sprinkling of Scripture*. I should have known better. Drawing, as with writing, turned out to follow this same principle (for me at any rate): The first draft is never the same as the finished product.

Meanwhile, I was taking one of my last classes at the University of Wisconsin—Eau Claire (UWEC)—an independent study on the Shinto Religion of Japan. At one point, I was given liberty to bring Japanese art books and art supplies to class. I thought it would be fun to create some of our own "Japanese" masterpieces. We had a great time drawing, painting, and being amazed at the talent that surfaced in the room; it was there that I discovered tempera paints. Later, at home, I recreated all of the artwork for *Rainy Day Haikus with a Sprinkling of Scripture* using tempera paints instead of colored pencils and found it a more satisfying medium with which to work for this particular project.

Also, while studying the Shinto Religion, we learned that many aspects of Japanese life and culture are grounded in this belief system. Simply put, Shinto is a belief in the gods called Kami, and purity—of place and person—is a very important aspect of worship. Culturally, this idea of purity and simplicity is found in everything from the way Japanese homes are kept, to the lines found in their architecture and paintings, and to the poetry we know today as Haikus.

Haiku poetry was born out of a style of poetry called Tanka; a form of poetry practiced in the Japanese courts prior to the 12th century. Tanka was constructed of five lines consisting of 5-7-5-7-7 syllables. Contests were often held with one person creating the first three lines of 5-7-5 syllables, while a second person would finish the poem with the last two lines of 7-7 syllables. As time passed by, the simplicity of the first three lines were distilled into complete poems and made popular by the three great masters of Haiku: Matsuo Basho, Yosa Buson, and Kobayashi Issa.[1]

Essentially, Haikus are written in a format of three lines consisting of 5-7-5 syllables. The language is simple and each Haiku includes a reference to the season; i.e., snow for winter, flowering crab trees for spring, etc. Haikus often contain a word that gives it a surprising turn in direction. This form of poetry is a way of writing about things in a manner that cuts out extraneous verbiage. It is a picture of life in its most refined telling; Haikus are often images of life that the rushing world has failed to see. It is a type of poetry that requires the reader to become involved, because a passive reading just will not suffice. This is why I love Haiku poetry.

*   *   *

One day last spring, I took a walk on the local walking trail. It looked like it might rain, so I grabbed my umbrella—just in case. I determined that I would look at everything to observe what I might not normally see. I did this with the idea that, afterwards, I would go home and write some Haikus. I wanted to distill what I saw with my eyes into images created with words. Fortunately, I had my umbrella because it did, indeed, rain! Not just a gentle spring rain, but at times a driving rain, with rain seemingly hurled out of the sky and dashed to the ground by the wind. It was exhilarating to be out there in the raw elements of wind and rain. The twenty-two Haikus in this book were born out of that walk on a rainy day.

Finally, while I immensely enjoyed the Religious Studies classes I took at UWEC, I hold to my faith in the God of Abraham, Isaac, and Jacob and His Word found in the Christian Bible. Believing that Jesus Christ is the Creator of rainy days, I was curious to see if I could find Scriptures that would complement the artwork and Haiku poetry in this book. Sure enough, I found in God's Word truth that completed this project; and that . . . is no small thing.

Come; go for a walk on a
rainy day with me . . .

Susan Steele

September 17, 2012

Come; go for a walk on a rainy day with me.

Venture out in your imagination
and be filled with

the images, sounds, and smells
of an early spring rain.

It's a lovely way to spend an afternoon . . .

The Lord has His way
in the whirlwind and
in the storm,
and the clouds are the
dust of His feet.
Nahum 1:3b

Rainy day walking

Drip, drizzle, pouring down rain

Rolling thunder booms

Darkened skies cloud filled

Rain drops dancing on the pond

Little bridge wet too

...I will give you rain
in its season, the land
shall yield its produce,
and the trees of the field
shall yield their fruit.
Leviticus 26:4

Walking trail wet

Rain drops collecting, pooling

Rivulets of water

Flowering crab trees

Delicate petals pressed down

In the dirt by rain

The tree grew and
became strong;
its height reached
to the heavens,
and it could be seen to
the ends of all the earth.
Its leaves were lovely...
Daniel 4:11-12a

Up and down my spine

Caused by thunder booming loud

Delicious shivers

The woods around me

Silent, deep, and still—quiet

Dripping spring green leaves

Ponder the path
of your feet,
and let all your ways
be established.
Proverbs 4:26

Another pathway

Into the woods disappears

Not for me today

Poor dandelion

Much maligned little flower

Pretty yellow face

Whatever the Lord
pleases He does,
in heaven and in earth...
He makes lightning for
the rain;
He brings the wind out of
His treasuries.
Psalm 134:6a, 7b

Purple lilacs bloom

Heavenly scented flower

Scent tickles my nose

Sky grows darker now

Wind gushes and blows harder

Lightning comes with rain

He is the Rock.
Deuteronomy 32:4a

Big black boulders hulk

Amid the sea of green grass

Seemingly misplaced

Umbrella held tight

No trees now, just a field

Only halfway home

And I said, "Oh that I
had wings like a dove!
For then I would fly
away and be at rest.
I would hasten my escape
from the windy storm
and tempest."
Psalm 55:6,8

Up ahead more trees

Following the river way

Shelter from the storm

Rain drops madly tossed

Hurled randomly—scattered

Soaking through and through

I will give you the
treasures of darkness
and hidden riches of
secret places,
that you may know that
I, the Lord,
who call you by your
name,
am the God of Israel.
Isaiah 45:3

Under trees still wet

No shelter here, too much rain

Sky looks lighter though

Black gnarled old tree

Silent river sentinel

Spooky in this light

Uphold my steps in
Your paths,
that my footsteps
may not slip.
Psalm 17:5

Rain drops disappear

Into the rushing river

Cycle completed

Sandy river bank

Re-sculpted by falling rain

Footprints left by me

The flowers appear on
the earth;
the time of singing
has come,
and the voice of
the turtledove
is heard in our land.
Song of Solomon 2:12

Breathe deep the fresh air

Pine scented, musky earth smell

Rain nearly stopped now

Little violet

Hiding amidst grass and trees

Rain washed purple face

My beloved spoke,
and said to me:
"Rise up, my love,
my fair one,
and come away.
For lo, the winter
is past, the rain is
over and gone.
Song of Solomon 2:10–11

Step out of the woods

Sun peeks through the clouds, rain stops

Robin looks for worms

Ready to go home

No more rainy day walking

Time to write haikus

About the Author

Susan Steele is a resident of Wisconsin and enjoys reading, photography, family tree research, and traveling. She is a graduate of the University of Wisconsin—Eau Claire (2012) and is involved in ministry as a teacher of the Old Testament Hebrew Bible. Susan is published in a poet's anthology titled Poetic Voices of America, Spring 1994, and is listed in the 2011 book of Who's Who Among Students in American Universities & Colleges. This is her first book of illustrated poetry.

Bibliography

Addiss, S., Yamamoto, F., & Yamamoto, A. (1998). *Haiku people: Big and small in poems and prints.* New York: Weatherhill, Inc.

Haas, R. (Ed.). (1994). *The essential haiku: Versions of Basho, Buson, & Issa.* New York: HarperCollinsPublishers.

Merrill, J. & Solbert, R. (Eds.). (1969). *A few flies and I: Haiku by Issa.* New York: Scholastic Book Services, a division of Scholastic Magazines, Inc., by arrangement with Pantheon Books.

Ryrie, C. (1985). *The Ryrie study bible: New King James Version.* Chicago: Moody Press.

Yamakage, M. (2006). *The essence of Shinto: Japan's spiritual heart.* New York: Kodansha International, Ltd.

Footnotes

[1] Patterns in Poetry: Haiku. (n.d.). Retrieved March 20, 2012, from http://www.cranberrydesigns.com/poetry/haiku/history.htm.

Look for Susan Steele's next book; a poignant autobiography of her family and how they endured the traumatic diagnosis of Alzheimer's and survived the subsequent downward spiral of her father's life as he succumbed to this devastating illness.

Alzheimer's:
The Story of a Family

Written and Compiled
By Susan Steele

Here are excerpts from *Alzheimer's: The Story of a Family*.

From birth to death
From death to birth
Life goes round
And round and round

You gave me birth
You watched me grow
You've held me, hugged me,
Rocked me, too

Life goes round
And round and round

I've watched you grow
I've held you, hugged you,
Rocked you, too

Life goes round
And round and round
From death to birth
From birth to death

By Susan Steele

The Story of a Man

Gary H. Steele, 63, of Black River Falls,
died Wednesday, January 28, 1998,
in the Tomah Veterans Administration
Medical Center.

Thus begins the obituary, the final summary, of
my father's life. Dad was diagnosed in May of 1988
with Alzheimer's disease; a debilitating illness that
robs one of memory, the ability to communicate, and
the remembrance of who's who. By January of 1990,
my mother had to let him go to the Veteran's Hospital
in Tomah. There he spent the final eight years of his
life—but that is not the sum total of a life lived. Here
is Gary's story . . .

On the day that Dad was buried it was bright,
sunny, and cold. It was a perfect, crisp winter day. We
listened to the words of comfort from the 23rd Psalm
and jumped at the ringing sound of shots fired from the
twenty-one gun salute that was his due. Mom received
the folded flag. As we stood there quietly for a moment,
moved by the realization that this was the end, we
were startled by the sound of shots fired over the hills

and then shouts from voices of people we could not see. Hunters. We looked at one another, smiled, and thought—what a perfect ending for a man who lived his life out-of-doors. It was a fitting tribute.

Funeral services for Gary H. Steele
were Saturday, January 31, 1998,
at 11 a.m. from the Buswell Funeral
Home. The Rev. Matthews officiated
and burial, with military honors,
was in the Trout Run Cemetery.

Thus ends the obituary, the final summary of my father's life. It was a life lived well.

Spirit Remains

A voice,
familiar laugh,
a pitch of sound,
stirs memories round.

A chance
encounter,
a silhouette,
palms, clammy wet.

I dream
a dream
of one I love,
memories spirited from above.[1]

By Betty J. Hembd Steele

Through the Eyes of a Wife

In Her Own Words:

Wednesdays Are For Gary . . .

He called me at work and asked, "What comes after 999?"

The answer should have been as easy as picking up the arrowheads he was cataloging, but, instead, he was calling me for the answer.

The frequent, foreboding conversations I had been having with close friends in the past few months were becoming a reality in this one question. Not that I hadn't seen some questionable activities in this same time period, but our days were stressful for other reasons, so it's easy to blame outside events.

1984-85 was a time of good-byes to many familiar people and things in our world. All three of our children left town to seek their own space: Susan, our oldest, was moving west to California. Walter, our second born, was going to a job near Madison, Wisconsin. Our youngest son, James, was graduating from high school and in a short time followed his brother to Madison.

We were also trying to sell the business we had operated the past 17 years. That was why I was working out—in anticipation of not working for ourselves anymore. So when Gary called me at work to ask about the next number after 999, I knew something aside from all the other stresses in our life was wrong.

That afternoon, I called our family doctor and filled him in on what had just happened and some of the other concerns I had about Gary's behavior. Such as, the lack of conversation this 'story-teller' was showing. As we sat at the local café over afternoon coffee he was starting to let me do all the talking. When friends joined us at the table he was giving nods and smiles to their questions instead of verbal answers. When a comment required an answer he was most often unable to supply the noun. He'd start talking and, if I understood what he wanted to say, I would fill in the noun for him and then he could continue his answer.

A medical appointment was made and his general health was checked over and the doctor asked him the questions in this little quiz; the questions we would hear again and again in the next year.

- How old are you?

  - 52.

- Where do you live?

- ■ Black River Falls.

- Where are you right now?

  - ■ At the clinic.

- Starting at 100, subtract the number 3 until you reach 7.

  - ■ 100, 97, 9 . . ., "I can't do that."

- Read the sentence on this paper and do what it says. The sentence read: Place this paper on the floor and pick it up again.

  - ■ Gary read it and did nothing.[2]

Bits and Pieces from Other Voices

Emily

Dear Grandpa,

Happy Birthday. Have a good time. I want you to go to sleep when it's dark. And when Grandma comes there she will give you a good night sweet kiss. And when you get better she will pick you up and get in the car and go home and watch TV and she will make you comfy in your chair.

Love, Emily

The love of a granddaughter towards her grandpa who is ill with Alzheimer's disease is very uplifting for the adults in the family dealing with the many sides of this devastating illness.

Emily Sue lives on the west coast, hundreds of miles from her Mid-west grandparents so she has learned early in her life what letters are all about. She "dictates" her letters to her mother who is instructed by this five-year-old daughter to write just what she says.

Many a letter comes showing the sensitivity of this very young writer, such as "and I really love you for a week," "and rainbows grow very tall and clouds grow very tall up in the sky," or her untimely "Happy Birthday" wishes. But the above letter to her grandpa was especially heart-rending to me as the wife working close with my ill husband. I know the wishes of Emily Sue cannot possibly come true, but way down deep in my heart it is the same wish I have carried since the diagnosis of "probable Alzheimer's Disease" was made and Emily's grandpa had to be placed in a constant care facility.

Our three children, in their mid-to-late twenties have created a stronghold for our family in their willingness to talk and to share their many feelings about the Alzheimer's disease. Although I have lost my husband's listening ear and shoulder, I have never really felt too alone because of the children's interaction. All three live a long distance away, but I feel a letter such as the one from Emily Sue says we have done well in our communications with each other. In our sharing, the grandchildren learn what caring is all about on a very personal level.

I thank you Emily Sue, for your good wishes. Grandpa no longer understands what is being read to him, but I know he feels the love. So, Grandpa, Dad, and Husband, we really love you for a week—every week, and may your rainbows glow against the clouds in the sky.[3]

Betty Hembd Steele
October 1991

Epilogue
Winter Is Over

For as long as stones survive on earth

And stars shine like diamonds in the sky

May our friendships never die.

And when the world is dark and gray

Least we not forget to pray

And thank the Lord for friends that stay.[+]

By Gary H. Steele
1974

Developmental Psychology has expanded its definition of development to include all the years of a person's life. Lifespan development researchers agree that growth and change do not happen only in the first thirteen years of a person's life. Of course, those of us who have lived beyond those years know that we continue to grow and change into our twenties, thirties—right on into middle and old age.

What is life but a series of seasons. Some are long and encompass many years and others are short—a few months, a year. The seasons of our life may be filled with great joy, life changing events, the totally unexpected, and the touch of sorrow. The environment that we live in and the experiences we live through mold us and make us into the people we are today.

In the writing of this book I have been touched by a deeper understanding of my mother's life. Through the sharing of her journal entries, her stories, and memories, I began to see those years of Dad's illness through her eyes. Her life was filled for a time with a very painful season . . .

Be sure to look for the book, *Alzheimer's: The Story of a Family*, to find out the rest of the story!

Footnotes

[1] This poem was written by my mother, Betty Steele, after my Dad passed away.

[2] This excerpt titled "Wednesdays Are For Gary . . ." was taken from the personal journals of my mother, Betty Steele.

[3] This excerpt titled "Emily" was taken from the personal journals of my mother, Betty Steele.

[4] This poem was written by my father, Gary Steele, in 1974.